Poem

Verbiage

Volume 1

Failure   Faith   Love

Introduction

Some people ask when and where did you find out you were a poet? Well, when I was real young, me and someone that was really special to me would battle sending poetry back and forth through letters. I then knew I was real good with words, but it was not until I was in my 20's that I really started to write. I started reading first. When I would read I could not put the book down and that is what really encouraged the writing. Now it's just habit when I hear a topic or I feel down or even when I'm at my best. The words, they just come like water and if I don't write it

Failure   Faith   Love

down then I'll lose it all. My collection of poetry is

called *Poem Verbiage*. It wasn't until I joined the

Muskogee Soul Searchers and I am now, called

a poet.

   KeyaSoul

Failure   Faith   Love

Vol. 1 Contents

Failure   Faith   Love

About the Author

Hello! I am Temarkeya Oliver. My friends

and family call me, Keya. Throughout life we go

through ups and downs, but I would like to

encourage you to keep your head to the hills from

which cometh our help. It takes Failure, Faith, and

Failure   Faith   Love

Love to overcome defeat. I would like to First

and foremost thank God for giving me the words

to speak and write. Secondly, shout out to my

family and my friends for your encouragement

along the way.

        Thank You!

Failure   Faith   Love

Today Is the Day

Today is the day

where I blow your email up with sentimental

gestures to show my love

Today is the day

I remember why I have fallen in love with a man

from the time we first met till now

Today is the day

where you see the love all over me, in my eyes

the glow on my face, through my warm embrace

Today is the day

where we stop and thank God for he brought us

together, made us for each other

Today is the day

where I'm giggly; I blush when you kiss me

Oh how I love to look into your brown eyes

~Temarkeya B~ 9

Failure   Faith   Love

Today is the day

where the love that we have fought for shows up

amongst us, creates the fire within us

and it never burns out

~Temarkeya B~ 10

Just When I thought

Just when I thought it was over for me,

Tragic

Just when I thought I would never see,

Blinded

Just when I thought there was no hope for me
Hopeless

Just when I thought the storm over powered me

Trials

Just when I thought love wasn't for me

Heartless

Just when I thought I was about to lose my mind
Brain-dead

Just when I thought I could never make it

He had a ram in the bush

I saw it when it came at me so fast

it knocked me over

I stumbled to the ground

with grace before me

~Temarkeya B~ 11

Failure   Faith   Love

He picked me up

Dusted me off

Mercy grabbed me

just in time

Favor was upon me

It took tragedy

blindness

lack of hope

heartache

and confusion

to see what God had waiting for me

~Temarkeya B~ 12

Failure   Faith   Love

My Being

It was never said that

I would be what you wanted me to be

It was written I'd be who I am supposed to be

I may never walk in your shoes

I may never swim the great big ocean or talk just
like you

But what I will do, is be my best at living in my own
skin

My very own being

Failure   Faith   Love

I Chose Life

The color of your skin never mattered

So what, you failed time and time again

You win some

You lose some

You get back up and fight some more

Don't look back

The door to success is now open

Go

Fight

Pray and Win

One day you will remember this time in life

Thank God

He brought you back

Failure   Faith   Love

The Fight

See it was neither ten feet, nor fifty

but one hundred feet back, just to gain twenty

She began to walk dragging one side of her body

Turmoil and pain claimed the left side of her body

Encouragement and who she really was

claimed the right side

She started to hide behind this old worn down tree

She was scared of hurt, pain, and making bad

choices

One day the tree and a strong ora of wind knocked

her on her butt

She then jumped up

Dusted off for another round, to war up and win

But she thought to herself, was it just the wind?

How she fell?

Why did she always fail?

Question after question

"Why," never mattered

It's the fight bestowed within you

that determines, how you get back up

That's what really matters

~Temarkeya B~ 15

Rain Storm

I'm going through it this morning

I got ran up on this morning

Fist fight

I lost a child this morning

Legacy broken

A storm cloud rained down on me this morning

God still had me covered

After the storm was over my face was drenched
with tears

I remembered who I was when I started

Who I am now and who I will be when this is over

A new color added to the rainbow

The darkest fuchsia

My footprint's unwashed

~Temarkeya B~ 16

Failure   Faith   Love

My Brother's Keeper

Like a knife through my heart

My life crushed from abandonment and death

All in one life sentence

Pushed to live and not die

Taught to be the best

Raised to be nothing but successful

Given the knowledge to be powerful

Knowledge is power

Smarter than average but at times often clueless

Drugs killed your brain

But you're still holding it together

It's better to be shot down with a bb gun than
killed with a bow and arrow

Someday you will find your way

I am my brother's keeper

~Temarkeya B~ 17

My Legacy Starts with Me

Down in the deeps of the bottom of the sea

You'll see the beautiful pools of fish that stick
together

In the country you will see the big red ants

They work day in and day out

My legacy starts with me

Two people

Women and Husband

Love and Wisdom

My legacy starts with me

Bound to do

Chosen to succeed

Known to be the greatest marathon runner

without running an official race

My legacy starts with me

Humpty dumpty sat on a wall

Off the wall he fell

It was the greatest fall

~Temarkeya B~ 18

Failure   Faith   Love

God always put me back together

After you fall

After you fail

After the rain

After the storm

You still have the power to win

My Legacy starts with me

~Temarkeya B~ 19

Failure   Faith   Love

Crying Jesus

Continuously at a loss for words

Speechless

Hurt but numb

Senseless

Nowhere to turn

Nowhere to run

No more hiding

Crying Jesus!

~Temarkeya B~ 20

Heartfelt

I'll love you when you have morning breathe or

even grow old and gray

I'll love you even when you fall down

I'll dust you off with nothing negative to say

I know you're not perfect

but you're well worth to have and to hold till death

You know those vows that will never tear us apart

Love

What is love?

Whatever you make it

I just want to love

Be loved

Never fail or fake it

It takes two people to hold a relationship together

One person to fail

Two people to love

One person to know

that it's the love

~Temarkeya B~ 21

Failure   Faith   Love

between two people

that is what brings out the best

among the two individuals

My heart bleeds love

When I think of you my heart feels loved

When I talk to you my heart knows love

Although I am absent from you my heart cries love

~Temarkeya B~ 22

Attracted to You

I'm attracted to your thoughts

Hearing you speak is like eating a catered meal

Come feed me

You're so intelligent

when I look in your eyes

I see a reflection of love

God made me for you

I'm totally turned on by your manly approach

I want more of your passion

I want you bad as ever

On another level

The love I have for you

was established at such a valuable time

Something like fine china or

a 1967 bottle of dark wine

Expensive, hard to obtain

But with each year

Each season

~Temarkeya B~ 23

Failure   Faith   Love

You bring that fire of mystery

If I was Bonnie

I would call you my Clyde

You found me

~Temarkeya B~ 24

I Was Wondering

I was wondering if you'd let me hold you

and give you something you could feel

I'm not talking the normal sexual favors

I am speaking a chance of a lifetime with me

That's the ordeal

A second chance of happiness

I'll even teach you a new dance

A lover's grove

Feel my heart beat up against yours

You're my rhythm and blues

It takes two

Two to commit

Two to love

Two to care

But it will be three, God, You, and Me

~Temarkeya B~ 25

Chosen

Hood girl, I love how you were down for the cause

City girl, I love how you raised him

Country girl taking over now

Early in the morning in the kitchen preparing food
for the soul

Mid-day on the dish board washing clothes

Pity parties from love

No time for that

I thought you knew Black Cinderella is back

I'm claiming my shoes although my heel is broke

Running too fast

I damaged one and lost the other

He ran after me like no other

He was something more to me than just

Prince Charming

He makes me faint

With those tender kisses

Down on one knee he looked up at me

I'm Chosen

~Temarkeya B~ 26

One of those Days

This is one of those days

Where I wish I could lay with you all day

This is one of those days

Where the words you say are replaying through my

head on repeat all day

This is one of those days

Where my thoughts of you won't go away

This is one of those days

Where my love for you grows deeper

Oh! How I long for your sweet caring hugs and

tender kisses

This is one of those days

Where my heart weeps from missing you

This is one of those days

I wish to share with you

You know one of those days

~Temarkeya B~ 27

Failure   Faith   Love

where we kick back at the park

Pack up a picnic basket of goodies and

share with one another

So caught up into each other all we notice is

how much our love has grown for one another

This is one of those days

Special days, we will think about

when we get older

~Temarkeya B~ 28

What is Sexy?

No one ever said you had to undress or be in a sex

moment just to be called sexy

What is Sexy?

Sometimes it's the softness of your skin, the bones

that highlight your smile, or just your love that

comes from within

Often it's the way you walk and the way you may

talk, then again it could be the way you kiss or the

way you shake your hips

It may even be in a gentle kiss that makes you

break a sweat

Sexy is a word with several definitions

Sexy is the fire that burns within a person and it is

shown, seen or felt on the outside

~Temarkeya B~ 29

Baby I'm Sick...

I got the I love me some you flu

my heart is weak

at times I can't even speak

my body gets shakes

fever, fever, fever because I miss you, fever

I can't calm my temperature down

I love me some you

I think about how I want to be closer to you

I get these cold shakes

see my world is cold without you

Baby, I need my Gatorade

You

Your my fruit passion

pour it in my cup

with each sip I take

my heart start to pump

~Temarkeya B~ 30

Failure   Faith   Love

When we both collide

It's nothing but love

Your just enough

I just want to love you for who you are

no money

no fame

Just you

The man that makes me sane when I'm with you

Insane when I'm without you

Baby, I'm sick!

~Temarkeya B~ 31

Failure   Faith   Love

Dreams vs. Reality!

As long as I help someone along the way

then my living shall not be in vain..Although I

dreamed many dreams, sacrificed and even death

was within me, I still battle with winning, Reality is I

may never live the life of my dreaming super star

or become the wife of a man that loves me like I

love my art

I may never be over many things, travel the world

conquering time, Drinking the finest wine

surrounded by people who love me passed my

appointed time

Reality is Dreams are dreams

I may never be a woman at my full potential

Dreaming, but a woman with purpose fulfilled

living

~Temarkeya B~ 32

Failure   Faith   Love

Reality is faith is your mystery

Dreams are just a stagnant way of listening

without faith there's no sight in seeing

Dreams often leave you clueless

Reality wins. Faith is your mystery

~Temarkeya B~ 33

The "N' Word

People here the word nigga and lose it

What's the meaning of the word?

I mean we are no longer in slavery!

People will be at a gathering and one white person

come in and start dropping the N word and people

start to fighting

I just ask, Why?!

It's a word that leaves us helpless trying to dodge a

knife, it kicks right off cloud nine, fearless of this

thing called life

Black people be like, "what's up my nigga?"

to a fellow African Americans

then a white person be like, "you nigga..."

is there a difference?

I be like, "nigga please" sometimes myself...

Failure   Faith   Love

Will we ever know to just let it go and save

ourselves?

no more, no more, We already passed the "no I'm

not dumb test..."

Let's put the N word to rest!

My Soul Seasoning

See my souls seasoning relates to my Nana's Peach

cobbler

Some people call it a bowl of sin

but I say that's love sacrificed for a win

Dough rolled out, sprinkled with flour, molded and

cooked to perfection, my skins complexion

My souls season is Sweet, just a little bitter, like the

peaches without all the sugar, A bold taste that

hugs the tongue, no measurements that's how it's

all done

My soul is seasoned like cinnamon or nutmeg

peach cobblers fire, Did I say I was for hire?

My soul seasoning is perfected to reflect the village

that raised me

my souls peach cobbler is the best

~Temarkeya B~ 36

Love

It exist today and yesterday

Can endure tomorrow and forever more

Trustworthy

Like the oceans breeze

Inhale

Exhale

Even like the deep sea

Transpires like the thoughts of a person

Constant

Remains like the air we breathe

Sometimes sweet

Sometimes hot

Sometimes cloudy

Like a strawberry shortcake

Fulfilling

Lasting

Calm like spring

Beautiful like summer

I am speaking of wonderful Love

~Temarkeya B~ 37

Passing Time

I'm kind at times

Funny when I'm chilling

Pretty cool in the Spring

Laid back in the summer

But if I find out you pulling a fast one,

I can and will go from 0 to 100

Ready to whoop your

Ask...

Me all your questions

I'll tell you no lies

Snakes dance with their eyes

Leaving you color blind

There's really only one thing

I have in mind,

To stand in line

At Braums...

~Temarkeya B~ 38

Failure	Faith	Love

Eat my ice cream

This too shall pass...

Nothing but time!

In life we will be faced with obstacles, backstabbing

people, people who accuse you of things, always

keep your cool and find a stress reliever that helps

you.

Failure   Faith   Love

Women

Women

We are crystals

When poured into a glass were something potent

We are generation XYZ

Chromosomes from our father and our mother

when combined together

Making Queens

Who are we?

Winners

We all know it

Sometimes we struggle

We're not the glass that holds up a TV

See through

We are the wires and when added to another wire

We're the sizzles, making electricity

Chemistry

Biology

A priceless worth

A hidden biography

~Temarkeya B~ 40

Failure   Faith   Love

We have along with others, cleaned ass

I mean glass

Took out trash

Even been called the underclass

We are women made to last

Villages raised us

We raise villages

Off gumbo

Fine picked peaches

We are the reason

The seasoning

The medicine

To this world

To this man's land

Who are we?

Women!

No Prayer, No Power

No prayer...no Power

Little prayer...little power

Lots of prayer...Power!

Failure   Faith   Love

Living or Existing?

At times I feel, I'm just existing

Making decisions

But who's really listening?

Are you Living or existing?

Existing in the shadows

Of others

Feeling real shallow

Only to find yourself

Waking up doing the same thing daily

existing

Off balance

Wishing and dreaming

Dreaming and wishing

Of your own plan to win

Are you living or existing?

Because of God's plan for my life

~Temarkeya B~ 43

Failure   Faith   Love

I win

Don't be afraid to just exist

When time comes

You will experience

What it is to be living

No longer just existing...

I bet that's how David felt, when he defeated

Goliath

God prepared him to Win

That purpose fulfilled living!

Stay True To You...

I figured out,

I'm ok with it

My story had to change

People

It wasn't the people

Well you believe in second chances right?

Don't follow humans

That will land you right in prison

Feeling like someone put a gun to my head

And all I have is one freedom call

Feeling like my dreams are all going to different

paths

It's too hard to walk away

Or take my sweat back

You know

Winners write history

~Temarkeya B~ 45

Failure   Faith   Love

Feeling as if I'm destined for greatness

But disturbed by hate

So I been pulling 720's

Circle after circle

Only to find my story changed

Because I wasn't being true to myself

The truth set me free...

Failure   Faith   Love

Still Pushing

I'm pushing to stay in my own narrow lane

Ride an ultimate rushing Long Beach California

wave

I'm pushing to say less

Achieve more

I'm pushing to be better

Pray more

Cuss a little less

Be my own guest

Showing love

Putting all bull stuff to rest

Taking the road less traveled is no fun

But rams in the bush

Blessings upon blessings

Have kept me in a race

Only I could run

Failure   Faith   Love

I have been push to say today

What you feed yourself daily

That's what you become...

~Temarkeya B~ 48

Faith Out My Pocket

I finally took my faith out my pocket

Sky rocketing like a rocket

I finally said, NO

To sinking sand

And yes to my Gold mine

My foundation

Built

From these

Once

Sinful hands

I finally took my faith out my pocket

Again

Ready to war up for another win

Leaving some standing behind me in the wind

Finally knowing who I am

I finally took my faith out my pocket...

~Temarkeya B~ 49

Failure   Faith   Love

I finally said, No

To someone's else's sinful nature

That rubs you the wrong way

Bonds you in tears

Feeling like

A creature from another galaxy

I finally took my faith out my pocket

And saw this rare piece of gold

A little dull

But still shining

And note came with it

You are my child

A chosen one

A piece of gold

Live right

I'll supply all your needs

My faith remains out my pocket!

~Temarkeya B~ 50

My Testimony

Would you mind if I reminisce over my life?

I cried the tears

Of women scorned for years

Confused

Misused

Lost time and even abused

Ridiculed for being who I am

When all I wanted to be was superwoman

What God has for you

Is for you

And you can't walk in my shoes

But listen to my testimony

I'm no longer that woman

I let go of the pain

I let go of the strain

I let go of the hurt

~Temarkeya B~ 51

Failure   Faith   Love

Now I know my worth

I let go and let God

He gives me peace of mind..

Need to Get My Life Right Now

Every time I think of how I used to be

That was then

Look at me now

I'm glad I'm not where I used to be

Thank God

He kept me

I used to be so foolish

A change has come over me

I must...

I need to get my life right, now

Change me, Oh God

I need to get my life right, now...

There comes a point in your life where all failures

and the love of God come together and you start to

get your life right. The windows of Heaven open up

and pour you out a blessing you're unable to

receive. Praise God, Get your life right!

~Temarkeya B~ 53

Failure   Faith   Love

Real feelings

You been so good

You been so kind

You been my friend

You been my piece of mind

When I think of things You done for me

My soul Cries

Thank You

Thank You

THANK YOU

Testimony after testimony

Even when I thought I was lonely

You been so Good

You been so kind

~Temarkeya B~ 54

Praise It Up

Sending up some praise

Praising it up

Last time I checked

I was in good health

Last time I checked my family was real rich,

Blessing on blessings

Heavenly mansion's

Let me shout this

God, you're the BEST...

Off the top of the brain just like that...

Failure   Faith   Love

What Path Do You Take?

Don't stare at four walls daily

Wondering if you will ever make it

Infuse your mind with positivity

Just like the Thrill of Mary's newborn baby

Be an activists

Not a bystander

Waiting on someone else to make the right move

That only lands you still waiting

To be your own you

Be your own boss

incline your mind with knowledge

That's gets you through this life biology

Lifeology

What path do you really take daily?

Failure   Faith   Love

In The Midst

But in the midst of all that

God still raised a champion!

Raised up for his Glory

Living miracle

Living testimony

Sacrificed

And at times

Only had bologna

To eat

Trust and believe

He always made a way

Tried

Tested

Almost died

But lived to say this one thing

Failure   Faith   Love

There is a living powerful God

Makes sure now, when it's all said and done

that your soul ain't in hell on fire!

~Temarkeya B~ 58

My Destiny

Retrieving my destiny

Never letting this whole life thing

get the best of me

Pulling out my guns, putting on the whole armor of

God, so my peace is real steel

Do you not understand?

Misery loves company

Retrieving my destiny

Boss hogging my way up

Switching lane to lane, Journey to journey

On the straight and narrow

Daily Dodging fiery darts and arrows

Some thought I lost, but no

it just pays a cost, to be a boss!

~Temarkeya B~ 59

Tough Skin

Tough skin

Newborn baby

Born to win

    Skin

Alligator in a swap

Trap house

Terminator like

    Skin

I won't give up

Failure not an option

Black never cracks

    Type skin

Church girls rock

I will give it all I got

Faith this thang out

Till the day I die

Loving the skin I'm in...

Failure   Faith   Love

Real Women

Real Women Boss up daily!

Her family calls her blessed...

Although in the past, she may have been a mess

But there's only one real judge

That gives new life Abundantly

She checks the mail frequently

All the Bill's are due

Her kids have talking shoes

Coats to little

And Pants that are now high waters too

A mother's blues

Today she noticed one roll of tissue

And the last of the toothpaste

She literally had to cut it open

The kids looked at her crazy

But she showed them how you make it do

~Temarkeya B~ 61

Failure   Faith   Love

what it do

Then go out and talk sophisticated

They win

She wins

Real mothers boss up daily

After a long day at work

She comes in prepares a meal

Not thinking of the not so good day

she may have had

She sat on the couch

Saw a mouse

Feel to sleep

Burned the cornbread

So she ran out to the store

Grab mouse traps

Forgot the cornbread to go with the Hamburger

stew

~Temarkeya B~ 62

Failure   Faith   Love

Got the tissue and toothpaste

Arrives back home

One of the kids greet her

Saying

"Mom"

"Can you help me with this project?"

Real moms boss up daily

Real wives boss up daily

She turned over to her husband

Who knew exactly what she needed

Him to hold her

Show her love

Encourage her

It's so motivating

Support is the best thing

Remembering not to neglect each other

Real women aren't loved daily!

~Temarkeya B~ 63

My Victory

21 Salvage said...

"I made it through the storm and now I'm a G"

Although, I never spent a day in the life of a

gangsta

I'm truly a gangsta at battling through this life

thang

That makes me a G

God's child

You see the storm and the rain

used to make me so weak

Just like losing a loved one

You barely even want to speak

You barely can eat

One thing you will never hear of me

Failure	Faith	Love

is that I lost a battle

I will always claim

My Victory...

I love you for so many reasons!

Poem

Verbiage I

I would like to thank God first for giving me the mind, thoughts, and writing ability to put it down on paper. Poem Verbiage I is a collection of poems that were written to express that we all have down falls, but we have to get back up and love is what makes up better.

www.ingramcontent.com/pod-product-compliance
Lightning Source LLC
Chambersburg PA
CBHW020605030426
42337CB00013B/1223